THE COOK'S COLLECTION

PARTY TREATS & SNACKS

Party Treats/Grange

Author: Annette Wolter
Photography: Susi and Pete Eising, Odette Teubner,
    Rolf Feuz and Karin Messerli
Translated by UPS Translations, London
Edited by Josephine Bacon

CLB 4158
This edition published in 1995 by Grange Books
an imprint of Grange Books PLC, The Grange, Grange Yard, London SE1 3AG
This material published originally under the series title "Kochen Wie Noch Nie"
by Gräfe und Unzer Verlag GmbH, München
© 1995 Gräfe und Unzer Verlag GmbH, München
English translation copyright: © 1995 by CLB Publishing, Godalming, Surrey
Typeset by Image Setting, Brighton, E. Sussex
Printed and bound in Singapore
All rights reserved
ISBN 1-85627-770-4

THE COOK'S COLLECTION

❋

PARTY TREATS
&
SNACKS

Annette Wolter

Grange
BOOKS

Introduction

Whether you are planning some interesting canapés to serve with drinks at a small get-together, or want to put together an attractive buffet for a larger party, you will find plenty of new ideas for colourful and tempting snacks in this collection of recipes. With the help of this book, you can really impress your friends with your newly extended repertoire of delicious bites.

When planning a party buffet, although it is tempting to prepare small quantities of several different dishes, you will invariably find that many of your guests will want to try a little of everything, and there will not be enough to go round. It is far easier in the long run to make larger quantities of a smaller selection of snacks. If you make an initial selection of just a few central dishes, you can then back them up with salads and breads to add flavour, texture and volume.

Party dishes should always be attractively presented, with great emphasis placed on freshness of tastes and colours. Above all, the real secret of a successful buffet is managing to avoid those dishes that need last-minute preparation. By preparing in advance you can ensure that you are free to enjoy the evening with your guests.

These recipes will provide you with the inspiration needed to create appetizing and original snacks for countless occasions, and will earn you praise from guests in the process.

Chicken and Fennel Tartlets

To make 6
400g/14oz fennel
125ml/4fl oz chicken stock
400g/14oz cooked boneless chicken
1 tbsp olive oil
1 tbsp lemon juice
1 tbsp mayonnaise
½ tsp mild paprika
Pinch of cayenne
1 lemon

For the Pastry:
100g/4oz butter, diced
200g/7oz wholemeal flour
Pinch of ground aniseed
Pinch of ground fennel seeds
½ tsp baking powder
Salt and freshly ground pepper
2 x size 3 eggs, lightly beaten

Preparation time:
1½ hours
Nutritional value:
Analysis per tartlet, approx:
• 1600kJ/380kcal
• 18g protein
• 22g fat
• 27g carbohydrate

Make a dough with the butter, flour, aniseed, fennel seeds, baking powder, a pinch of salt and pepper and the eggs. Knead lightly until smooth. Trim and wash the fennel, reserving the feathery leaves. Cut the fennel into matchstick strips. • Place the chicken stock in a pan, bring to the boil and add the fennel strips. Lower the heat, cover and simmer for 15 minutes. Drain and set aside. • Grease 6 x 8cm/3 inch tartlet tins. • Roll out the dough on a lightly floured work surface. Cut out 6 circles, slightly larger than the tins. Line the tins with the dough circles, prick the bases, and bake in a preheated oven at 180°C/350°F/gas mark 4 for 15 minutes. • Remove the pastry cases from the tins and transfer carefully to a wire rack to cool. • Dice the chicken and mix with the fennel, oil, lemon juice, mayonnaise, paprika and cayenne. • Slice the lemon. • Fill the tartlet cases with the chicken and fennel mixture, and garnish with the lemon slices and reserved fennel leaves.

Beetroot Canapés

250g/8oz beetroot
1 onion
2 tbsps olive oil
1 tsp caraway seeds
½ tbsp vegetable stock granules
Pinch powdered cloves
Pinch ground allspice
4 tbsps crème fraîche
Juice ½ lemon
1 tsp grated horseradish
4 slices mixed grain bread
10g/¼oz softened butter
1 tbsp chopped chives
50g/2oz Emmental cheese

Preparation time:
30 minutes
Cooling time:
30 minutes
Nutritional value:
Analysis per serving, approx:
• 110kJ/260kcal
• 8g protein
• 14g fat
• 26g carbohydrate

Peel the beetroot, rinse and grate coarsely. Peel the onion, chop finely and fry in the oil until it becomes soft. • Add the beetroot, caraway seeds, stock granules, powdered cloves and allspice. Pour in half a cup of water and cook for 15 minutes stirring frequently. • Add the crème fraîche to the vegetables. Season the beetroot with the lemon juice and horseradish. Leave to cool. • Butter the bread thinly and then spread with the cooled beetroot mixture. Sprinkle over the chopped chives and decorate with triangles of Emmental cheese.

Cottage Cheese and Herb Canapés

2 shallots
500g/1lb 2oz low-fat cottage cheese
2 tbsps sesame oil
Juice 1 lemon
2 tsps mild mustard
2 tsps honey
1 tsp seasoned salt
3 pinches white pepper
Several sprigs of mixed herbs, eg. parsley, dill, lovage
Some watercress leaves, nettle leaves and/or marigold petals
2 slices wholemeal bread
2 slices mixed grain bread
4 slices rye bread
10g/¼oz butter
2 carrots
½ cucumber (about 200g/7oz)
2 green sweet peppers
Some radishes
1 tbsp dried yeast
1 tbsp sesame seeds

Preparation time:
40 minutes
Nutritional value:
Analysis per serving, approx:
• 1675kJ/400kcal
• 26g protein
• 9g fat
• 56g carbohydrate

Peel the shallots and chop finely. Mix the cottage cheese with the oil, lemon juice, mustard, honey, seasoned salt, pepper and chopped shallots. Rinse the herbs, pat dry and chop, leaving aside one or two leaves and sprigs for the garnish. Add the chopped herbs to the creamed cottage cheese. • Spread a thin layer of butter on each slice of bread, and then a much thicker layer of the cream. • Rinse and peel the carrots, then grate coarsely. Cover the two slices of mixed grain bread with grated carrot. • Peel the cucumber, slice thinly and arrange on the wholemeal bread. • Rinse the peppers, halve, remove the seeds and stalk and cut into thin strips. Arrange on two slices of the rye bread. • Cut the radishes into wafer-thin slices and arrange on the remaining rye bread slices. • Lightly toast the dried yeast and the sesame seeds. Sprinkle the yeast flakes over the carrot topping and the sesame seeds over the other toppings.

Caviar Canapés

To make 8:
8 baguette slices
125g/5oz Mascarpone
2-3 tbsps milk
125g/5oz red caviar
2-3 dill leaves

Preparation time:
20 minutes
Nutritional value:
Analysis per serving, approx:
• 590kJ/140kcal per canapé
• 6g protein
• 6g fat
• 13g carbohydrate

Toast the bread. • Mix the milk with the Mascarpone and spoon it into a piping bag with a star nozzle. Pipe it around the edge of the bread and then place a teaspoon of caviar in the middle. Garnish with a small sprig of rinsed dill.

Garlic Croûtons

To make 8:
4 tbsps olive oil
3 garlic cloves
8 baguette slices
1 hard-boiled egg
2 tomatoes
8 anchovy fillets
1-2 tsps lemon juice
Salt and freshly ground black pepper
1 tbsp chopped chives

Preparation time:
20 minutes
Nutritional value:
Analysis per croûton, approx:
• 540kJ/130kcal
• 5g protein
• 6g fat
• 14g carbohydrate

Heat the oil in a large frying pan. Peel the garlic cloves and crush two cloves through a garlic press into the oil. Add the bread slices and fry on both sides over a medium heat until golden brown. Leave the croûtons to drain on kitchen paper. • Remove the shell from the hard-boiled egg. Place the tomatoes in boiling water for a few seconds, remove the peel, halve and seed. Add the egg, anchovy fillets and the third chopped garlic clove and purée in a liquidiser. Season with salt, pepper and lemon juice and then spread over the baguette slices. • Sprinkle chopped chives over the croûtons and serve.

Olive Tapas

To make 8:
1 maatjes herring fillet
100g/4oz green olives
100g/4oz black olives
Some parsley leaves
1 punnet cress
1 tsp mustard
1 tbsp olive oil
8 baguette slices
½ lemon

Preparation time: 20 minutes
Nutritional value:
Analysis per tapa, approx:
• 630kJ/150kcal
• 3g protein
• 9g fat
• 14g carbohydrate

Remove any bones from the maatjes herring fillet and stone the olives. Rinse the parsley and shake dry. Set one sprig aside for the garnish. Snip off the cress, rinse under the cold tap and drain. • Purée the maatjes fillet, olives, parsley and cress for a few seconds only, then stir in the oil and mustard. • Spread the purée on the bread. Peel the lemon and remove the pith, then slice it thinly, before cutting the slices into wedges. •Garnish the bread with lemon wedges and parsley.

Stuffed Eggs

8 eggs
1 small onion
2 celery stalks
Bunch dill
1 small gherkin
75g/3oz softened butter
½ tsp salt
1 tsp coarse French mustard
1 tsp paprika
2 tsp freshly grated horseradish
50g/2oz prawns
100g/4oz sliced smoked salmon
25g/1oz red caviar

Preparation time:
45 minutes
Nutritional value:
Analysis per serving, approx:
• 1600kJ/380kcal
• 23g protein
• 30g fat
• 7g carbohydrate

Pierce each egg with a needle and boil for 10-12 minutes. • Immediately immerse in cold water for a few moments, remove the shell and leave to cool. • Peel and chop the onion. Rinse the celery, drain and remove any coarse threads. Chop the celery first into thin slices and then into cubes. Rinse the dill, shake dry and chop finely. Reserve one sprig for the garnish. Dice the gherkin. • Cut the hard-boiled eggs in half lengthways. Ease out the egg yolks, place in a bowl and mash with a fork. Add the softened butter and season with the salt, mustard, paprika and horseradish. Stir in the onion, celery and dill. Transfer the egg-yolk mixture into a piping bag fitted with a star nozzle and pipe into the egg-white halves. Alternatively, simply spoon the mixture into the egg. •Arrange the egg halves on a serving dish. Rinse the prawns and pat dry. Surround the stuffed eggs with rolls of salmon. Top eight egg halves with the caviar and the rest with prawns. Garnish each one with a small sprig of dill.

Coriander Straws

To make 40 straws:
15g/½oz yeast
125ml/4fl oz lukewarm water
250g/8oz flour
125g/5oz softened butter
1 egg yolk
1 tsp salt
2-3 tbsps coriander seeds
1 egg
Salt
Butter for greasing

Preparation time:
20 minutes
Rising time:
1 hour
Baking time:
20 minutes
Nutritional value:
Analysis per serving, approx:
• 210kJ/50kcal per straw
• 1g protein
• 3g fat
• 5g carbohydrate

Crumble the yeast into lukewarm water, stir well, cover and leave for about 30 minutes. • Sift the flour into a bowl. Cut the butter into knobs and place around the edge of the flour with the salt and egg yolk. Pour the yeast in the middle. Stir first with a spoon and then knead to a smooth dough. Cover and leave at room temperature for 30 minutes. • Heat the oven to 200°C/400°F/gas mark 6 and grease the baking tray. • Roll out the dough on a floured work top into a sheet about 20cm/8 inches by 40cm/16 inches and to a thickness of about 1cm/½ inch. Cut fingers about 1cm/½ inch wide and then lay them out on the baking tray about 2cm/1 inch apart. Crush the coriander seeds using a pestle and mortar. Whisk the egg with some salt. Coat the straws with the egg and then sprinkle with the coriander seeds. Bake the straws in the oven for about 20 minutes or until golden.

Thyme Wafers

To make 80 wafers:
250g/8oz wholemeal wheat
250g/8oz wholemeal rye flour
2 tsps ground caraway seeds
2 tsps salt
2 tsps baking powder
4 tsps dried thyme
3 eggs
150g/5½oz butter
150g/5½oz margarine
1-2 bunches fresh thyme
Flour for the work top
Coarse salt
Caraway seed
Margarine for greasing

Preparation time:
30 minutes
Baking time:
15-20 minutes
Nutritional value:
Analysis per serving, approx:
• 210kJ/50kcal each
• 1g protein
• 3g fat
• 4g carbohydrate

Mix both types of flour with the caraway seeds, salt, baking powder and 2 teaspoons of crushed thyme leaves. Make a well in the middle, add two eggs and one egg white and mix in a little flour. Cut the butter and margarine into small knobs, mix with the flour and knead into a smooth dough. Break the dough into three pieces. Leave for about 15 minutes in a cool place. • Heat the oven to 200°C/400°F/gas mark 6 and grease two baking trays. • Roll out the dough to a thickness of about 2mm/⅛ inch. Use a pastry cutter to cut 2cm/1-inch wavy strips and then cut them into 10cm/4-inch lengths. Place the pastry fingers on the baking trays. Whisk the remaining egg yolk with a little water, and brush over the pastry. Sprinkle with the remaining thyme. Add a little coarse salt and caraway seeds if required. • Bake the thyme straws for 15-20 minutes on the middle shelf of the oven until golden and then leave to cool.

Cottage Cheese on Cucumber Slices

400g/14oz cucumber
½ tsp salt
200g/7oz small courgettes
2 tomatoes
1 onion
Some dill leaves
500g/1lb 2oz cottage cheese
1 tsp salt
Freshly ground white pepper
Pinch hot paprika

Preparation time:
40 minutes
Nutritional value:
Analysis per serving, approx:
• 1590kJ/380kcal
• 28g protein
• 25g fat
• 9g carbohydrate

R inse the cucumber thoroughly in lukewarm water and then cut it into 1cm/½-inch slices. Arrange them on a serving dish and sprinkle with salt. • Rinse the courgettes and cut them into small, even cubes. Score the skin of the tomatoes, dip them in boiling water for a few seconds, remove the skin and cut into quarters. Remove the midrib and cut into cubes. • Peel and chop the onion. Rinse the dill, shake dry and snip into small sprigs. Mix the chopped vegetables with the cottage cheese and then season well with salt, pepper and paprika. • Spoon the cottage cheese on to the cucumber slices and garnish each portion with a small sprig of dill. • Serve with buttered wholemeal rolls or pumpernickel.

Cottage Cheese with Herbs on French-bread Boats

1 garlic clove
Fresh herbs, e.g. dill, tarragon,
chervil, parsley, salad burnet,
rosemary, chives
1 large green pepper
400g/14oz French stick
500g/1lb 2oz cottage cheese
2 tbsps olive oil
1 tsp seasoned salt
100ml/3fl oz single cream

Preparation time:
40 minutes
Nutritional value:
Analysis per serving, approx:
• 1890kJ/450kcal
• 13g protein
• 15g fat
• 64g carbohydrate

Peel the garlic and chop finely. Rinse the herbs, shake dry, discard any thick stalks and chop finely. • Halve the pepper lengthways and remove the seeds, pith and stalk. Rinse the pepper halves, dry and cut into cubes. • Cut the French stick in half lengthways and then into even slices. Tear out and discard about two-thirds of the soft crumb. •Mix the cottage cheese with the oil, seasoned salt, chopped garlic, herbs and cream. Season well and then spoon the cheese topping on to the bread. Garnish each boat with a few pepper cubes.

Ham Croissants

To make 16 pieces:
50g/2oz low-fat cottage cheese
6 tbsps milk
5 tbsps oil
½ tsp salt
300g/10oz self-raising flour
250g/8oz Feta cheese
150g/5½oz raw ham
Bunch of fresh or 1 tsp dried thyme
Salt and freshly ground black pepper
1 egg yolk
1 tbsp milk
2 tbsps sesame seeds
Butter for greasing

Preparation time:
40 minutes
Baking time:
20-25 minutes
Nutritional value:
Analysis per serving, approx:
• 760kJ/180kcal per croissant
• 8g protein
• 10g fat
• 14g carbohydrate

Mix together the cottage cheese, milk, oil and salt. Stir the flour into the cottage cheese. Knead well. • Cut the feta cheese and ham into cubes. Remove the leaves from the fresh thyme or crush the dried thyme. Mix into the feta cheese and ham cubes. • Heat the oven to 200°C/400°F/gas mark 6 and grease the baking tray. • Roll out the dough on a floured work top. Cut out rectangles (14cm/6 inches x 12cm/4 inches) with a pastry cutter and halve each one diagonally. Place one tablespoon of the filling in each triangle and then roll into a croissant, pressing down the edges. Whisk the egg yolk with the milk and brush onto the croissants. Sprinkle with sesame seeds. • Place the croissants on the baking tray and bake for 20-25 minutes or until golden. • Serve hot or cold.

Caraway Rolls

To make 16 rolls:
250g/8oz wholemeal flour
10g/¼oz dried yeast
50g/2oz softened butter
1 tsp salt
1 egg
1 tsp each sweet paprika and
rose paprika
1 tsp dried thyme
125ml/4fl oz lukewarm milk
200g/7oz cooked ham without
rind
100g/4oz Feta cheese
2 tsps caraway seeds
2 bunches chives
Butter for greasing

Preparation time:
40 minutes
Rising time:
1½ hours
Baking time:
25 minutes
Nutritional value:
Analysis per roll, approx:
• 590kJ/140kcal
• 6g protein
• 7g fat
• 10g carbohydrate

Mix the flour with the yeast in a warm bowl. Cut the butter into knobs and add to the flour. Mix the milk with the salt, egg, paprika and thyme and pour into the flour. Knead well. Cover the dough and leave for 50 minutes to rise. • Chop the ham and cut the cheese into cubes. Add the caraway seeds. Rinse the chives, shake dry and chop. • Roll out the pastry on a lightly floured work top into a rectangle measuring 20cm/8 inches x 16cm/6 inches and to a thickness of about 1cm/½ inch. Spread the cheese and ham mixture evenly over the pastry sheet and sprinkle with the chopped chives. Roll up the pastry sheet and cut into 1cm/½-inch slices. • Place the rolls on a greased baking tray, cover and leave for a further 25 minutes. • Heat the oven to 200°C/400°F/ gas mark 6. • Bake for 25 minutes.

Stuffed Turkey Fillet

To serve 8:
400g/14oz spinach
2 onions
2 garlic cloves
1 thick slice stale bread, crusts removed
2 tbsps olive oil
50g/2oz freshly grated Parmesan cheese
50g/2oz cream cheese
1 egg
2 tbsps breadcrumbs
2 tbsps flaked almonds
½ tsp dried oregano
Pinch of ground nutmeg
Salt and freshly ground black pepper
1.5kg/3lbs 6oz turkey breast in one piece
½ tsp dried thyme
4 tbsps sunflower oil
125ml/4fl oz boiling water
200g/7oz mushrooms
2 shallots
15g/½ oz butter
2 tbsps finely chopped fresh parsley
250ml/8fl oz double cream
250ml/8fl oz crème fraîche

Preparation time:
1 hour
Cooking time:
1½ hours
Relaxing time:
6 hours
Nutritional value:
Analysis per serving, approx:
• 2500kJ/600kcal
• 54g protein
• 35g fat
• 16g carbohydrate

Trim and wash the spinach. Place in a pan and cook for 5 minutes in the water still clinging to the leaves. Drain, squeeze out excess water and finely chop. • Peel and chop the onions. Peel and finely chop the garlic. • Tear the bread into pieces and place in a bowl. Cover with cold water and set aside to soak. • Heat the olive oil, and fry the onion and garlic for 5 minutes or until transparent but not browned. Add the spinach, and stir-fry until all the liquid has evaporated. Transfer to a bowl. • Squeeze out the bread. Mix together the spinach, Parmesan

20

cheese, cream cheese, egg, breadcrumbs, flaked almonds, oregano and nutmeg, and season to taste with salt and pepper. • Wash the turkey breast and pat dry. Using trussing thread, sew up the places in the meat where the bones were removed. Cut a deep pocket in the meat and spoon in the spinach stuffing. Sew the meat together with trussing thread. • Rub with salt and pepper, sprinkle over the thyme and place in a roasting tin. • Heat the sunflower oil, and pour over the turkey. Roast in a preheated oven at 200°C/400°F/gas mark 6 for 1½ hours, frequently pouring a little hot water around the turkey and basting the meat with the roasting juices. • Remove the turkey from the roasting tin and wrap in foil. When cold, set aside in the refrigerator to rest for 6 hours. • Make the sauce. Thinly slice the mushrooms. Peel and finely chop the shallots. • Melt the butter, and stir-fry the mushrooms for 3 minutes over a high heat. Add the shallots and parsley, and stir-fry until browned. Season with salt and pepper to taste and remove from the heat. Stir in the cream and crème fraîche. Transfer to a sauce boat, cover and set aside in the refrigerator. • Remove the turkey from the foil and take out the trussing thread. Carve the turkey in thick slices and hand the sauce separately.

Cheese and Pine Nut Pie

Quantities for 1 26cm/10in pie:
300g/10oz frozen puff pastry
8 preserved vine leaves
1 leek
1 garlic clove
200g/7oz feta cheese
3 eggs
200g/7oz low fat curd cheese
100g/4oz full fat soft cheese
1 tbsp capers
½ tsp salt
20g/¾oz pine nuts
Butter for the pie dish

Preparation time:
40 minutes
Baking time:
50 minutes
Nutritional value:
Analysis per piece, if divided into 12 slices, approx:
• 1000kJ/240kcal
• 11g protein
• 17g fat
• 11g carbohydrate

Defrost the frozen puff pastry. • Wash the vine leaves and pat them dry on kitchen paper. Chop the leek. Finely chop the garlic. • Lay the sheets of pastry one on top of the other and roll them out to the shape of the quiche dish. Line the dish with the pastry and arrange the vine leaves on top. • Work the feta cheese through a sieve and mix into a creamy paste with the eggs, curd cheese, soft cheese, capers, salt, garlic and chopped leek. • Spread the mixture onto the vine leaves and sprinkle on the pine nuts. • Bake on the centre shelf of a preheated 200°C/400°F/Gas Mark 6 oven for 50 minutes; serve hot or cold.

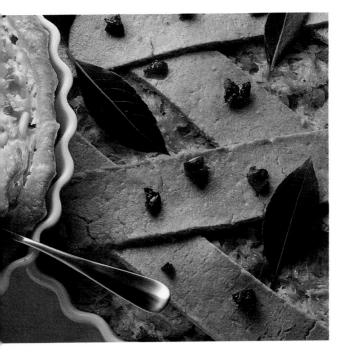

Sauerkraut Pie

Quantities for 1 32cm/12in pie:
350g/11oz floury potatoes
100g/4oz butter
200g/7oz buckwheat flour
30g/1oz soya flour
1 tsp sea salt
1¼ tsp baking powder
200g/7oz rindless streaky bacon
4 onions
4 tbsps sunflower oil
1kg/2¼ oz sauerkraut, rinsed
200g/7 fl oz sour cream
Pinch of black pepper
1 tsp sweet paprika
4 bay leaves
1 egg yolk
Butter for the quiche dish

Preparation time:
40 minutes
Cooking time:
40 minutes
Baking time:
35-40 minutes
Nutritional value:
Analysis per piece, if divided into 16 slices, approx:
• 1090kJ/260kcal
• 6g protein
• 19g fat
• 17g carbohydrate

Peel the potatoes and boil until soft, then mash with the butter. Mix the buckwheat flour and potatoes and combine with the soya flour, baking powder and salt, and knead together. • Dice the bacon and onions. • Fry bacon in the oil until crispy, put aside half of the bacon and mix the onion in with the rest; fry until golden. • Chop the sauerkraut. • Whisk the sour cream and spices and combine with the onion and bacon mixture, and the sauerkraut. • Butter the pie dish, pour in the sauerkraut mixture and add the bay leaves. • Roll out the pastry, cut into strips 4cm/2in wide, and lay these across the sauerkraut in a crisscross pattern. • Beat the egg yolk with a little water and use it to glaze the pastry. Press the remaining cubes of bacon into the glaze. • Bake the pie on the centre shelf of a preheated 200°C/400°F/Gas Mark 6 oven for 35 to 40 minutes.

Maatjes Herring Cocktail

4 maatjes herring fillets
150g/5 ½oz cooked celery
1 sharp apple
Juice of 1 lemon
2 hard-boiled eggs
2 tbsps wine vinegar
½ tbsp hot mustard
1 tbsp oil
1 finely chopped onion
1 tbsp tomato ketchup
Few drops of Tabasco sauce
Salt and pepper

Preparation time:
30 minutes
Nutritional value:
Analysis per serving, approx:
• 940kJ/210kcal
• 12g protein
• 14g fat
• 11g carbohydrate

Soak the fillets in water for 20 minutes, pat them dry and then dice them with the celery and the peeled apple. Sprinkle with the lemon juice. Mix the egg yolks with the other ingredients. • Coat the cocktail with the sauce and decorate with strips of egg white.

Stuffed Salmon Rolls

1 small sharp apple
1 hard-boiled egg
40g/1¼oz fresh horseradish
1 tbsp lemon juice
1 tbsp oil
5 tbsp single cream
Pinch each of salt and sugar
8 slices smoked salmon
Few oakleaf lettuce leaves
1 untreated lemon
1-2 dill sprigs

Preparation time:
20 minutes

Nutritional value:
Analysis per serving, approx:
• 1085kJ/260kcal
• 20g protein
• 16g fat
• 8g carbohydrate

Dice the egg, the peeled apple and horseradish, then blend them in a liquidiser with the oil and cream. Season the resulting purée and spread it on the salmon slices. Roll them up and arrange on lettuce leaves with lemon slices and dill.

25

Chicken Strudel

To serve 8:
2 x 1kg/2¼ lb chickens, with giblets
100g/4oz rindless smoked bacon
1 tsp dried thyme
1 tsp dried sage
Salt and freshly ground white pepper
100g/4oz mushrooms
10 large savoy cabbage leaves
2 eggs
2 tbsps finely chopped fresh parsley
125ml/4fl oz double cream
15g/½oz butter

For the Pastry:
300g/10oz flour
1 egg
Salt
125ml/4fl oz lukewarm water
1 tbsp sunflower oil
2 tbsps flour
75g/3oz butter

Preparation time:
1½ hours
Baking time:
30 minutes
Nutritional value:
Analysis per serving, approx:
• 3000kJ/710kcal
• 61g protein
• 40g fat
• 30g carbohydrate

Skin the chickens and remove the breasts. Cut the remaining meat from the bones and dice. • Trim the chicken livers. Wash, pat dry and dice. • Cut the bacon into 1cm/½-inch wide strips. Place the chicken and the bacon on a plate, sprinkle over the thyme and sage, and season to taste with salt and pepper. Set aside in the refrigerator for 30 minutes. • Finely slice the

mushrooms. Wash the cabbage leaves, pat dry and remove the stalks. • Make the pastry. Sift the flour onto a clean work surface. Add the egg, ¼ tsp salt and half the water, and knead into a smooth dough. Add a little more water, if necessary. The dough should be smooth and shiny. Shape the dough into a ball, brush with the oil, cover and set aside to rest for 30 minutes. • Put the chicken meat, apart from the breast, through a mincer twice, on its finest setting. • Put the minced meat in a bowl over ice cubes. Stir in the eggs, parsley and cream. Season to taste with salt and pepper. Cover and set aside over the ice for 30 minutes. • Cut the chicken breast into 2cm/3/4-inch wide strips. Melt the butter, and stir-fry the chicken breast and the livers and over a high heat for 2 minutes. Drain on kitchen paper and set aside. • Roll out the dough on a lightly floured work surface to a large, paper-thin square. Trim off any thick edges. Melt 50g/2oz of the butter and brush over the dough. • Spread half the chicken stuffing over the cabbage leaves. Place the strips of breast meat and the diced liver in the centre. Cover with the remaining stuffing. Place everything on the dough and roll up. • Shape the pastry roll into a horse shoe and lay on the baking sheet. Melt the remaining butter, and brush half of it over the pastry roll. • Bake in a preheated oven at 200°C/400°F/gas mark 6 for 30 minutes. • During the baking time, brush the pastry roll frequently with the remaining melted butter. • Cut the chicken strudel into 16 equal portions, and serve hot with a colourful mixed salad.

Trout Pâté en Croûte

To serve 6:

For the pastry:
350g/11oz flour
125g/5oz clarified butter
1 egg yolk
½ tsp salt
4-8 tbsps ice cold water
2 eggs, separated

For the filling:
6 fresh fillets of trout
200g/7oz plaice fillets
2 onions
15g/½oz butter
3 eggs
4 tbsps cream
2 tbsps breadcrumbs
½ tsp salt
Pinch each of freshly ground
white pepper and freshly grated
nutmeg
3 smoked trout fillets
1 bunch dill

Preparation time:
1¾ hours
Chilling time:
at least 5 hours
Baking time:
1 hour 20 minutes
Nutritional value:
Analysis per serving, approx:
• 1945kJ/465kcal
• 33g protein
• 22g fat
• 32g carbohydrate

To make the dough, sift the flour into a shallow bowl, make a well in the centre and place dots of clarified butter around the edge. Place the egg yolk in the well, add the salt and water and, making sure your hands are as cool and dry as possible, knead quickly. Form the dough into a ball and refrigerate for 5 hours, or

28

preferably overnight. • Wash and dry the trout and plaice, then cut them into fine strips. Chop the onion very finely and fry in the butter until transparent; leave the onion to cool. Mince the fish very finely in a mincer or food processor. Stir the eggs, cream and breadcrumbs into the fish, add the onions and season with salt, pepper and nutmeg. • Heat the oven to 200°C/400°F/Gas Mark 6. Butter a loaf tin. • Roll out the dough on a floured surface and cut out 2 rectangles the same size as the tin. Line the base of the pan with one of the rectangles. Line the sides with dough and seal the seams well. Fill the pastry case with half the filling, lay the smoked trout on top and sprinkle with chopped dill. Spoon in the remaining fish mixture. Make a few holes in the dough reserved for the lid with the tines of a fork, then place the lid over the filling. Seal firmly all round the edge. Use the remaining dough for decoration. •Separate the egg yolks and whites. Brush the decorations with lightly beaten egg white and lay them on the lid. Finally brush all over with beaten egg yolk. • Bake on the bottom shelf of the oven for 1 hour and 20 minutes. • Serve either hot or cold, with a fresh salad if desired.

Spinach and Cod Flan

To serve 6:
100g/4oz wholewheat flour
50g/2oz buckwheat flour
100g/4oz margarine
50g/2oz butter
200g/7oz low-fat quark
3 eggs
1 tsp garlic salt
½ tsp black pepper
Pinch grated nutmeg
400g/14oz spinach
600g/1lb 6oz cod fillet
1 tbsp lemon juice
½ tsp sea salt
150g/5½oz coarsely grated
Cheddar cheese
1 tbsp finely chopped fresh dill
25g/1oz butter, diced
1 bunch radishes

Preparation time:
30 minutes
Baking time:
40 minutes
Nutritional value:
Analysis per serving, approx:
• 2320kJ/555kcal
• 37g protein
• 35g fat
• 20g carbohydrate

Mix the flours with the margarine, butter, quark, eggs and seasonings. • Wash and pick over the spinach; set aside a few attractive leaves. Blanch the spinach for 1 or 2 minutes in boiling salted water, drain it, then chop it coarsely and mix into the dough. • Wash and dry the fish, cut it into 1cm/½-inch cubes, season with lemon juice and salt and mix into the dough. • Heat the oven to 200°C/400°F/Gas Mark 6. Butter a 28cm/11-inch springform tin. • Press the dough into the tin and bake for 30 minutes. • Mix the cheese with the dill and scatter over the flan; dot the top with butter and bake for another 10 minutes. • Leave the flan in the tin for 10 minutes before unmoulding. Garnish with radishes and spinach and serve.

Salmon Flan with Cheese

To serve 6:
4 eggs, separated
100g/4oz wholemeal flour
100g/4oz butter
200g/7oz low-fat curd cheese
1 tsp garlic salt
2 pinches white pepper
Pinch grated nutmeg
250g/8oz spinach
150g/5½oz smoked salmon
400g/14oz coley fillet
2 tbsps lemon juice
½ tsp salt
1 tbsp finely chopped fresh dill
250g/8oz Gouda cheese
100g/4oz Cheddar or
Cheshire cheese

For the garnish:
100g/4oz smoked salmon
slices
150g/5½oz full-fat quark
4 sprigs dill

Preparation time:
1 hour
Baking time:
35 minutes
Nutritional value:
Analysis per serving, approx:
• 2780kJ/665kcal
• 51g protein
• 43g fat
• 14g carbohydrate

Mix the egg yolks with the flour, butter, quark and seasonings. Blanch the spinach and chop it coarsely. Shred the salmon. Mix these into the dough. • Dice the fish fillets and sprinkle them with lemon juice, salt and dill. • Coarsely grate 150g/5½oz of the Gouda cheese and cut the rest into strips. Beat the egg whites until stiff. Mix the diced fish and grated cheese into the beaten egg. Heat the oven to 200°C/400°F/Gas Mark 6. • Grease a springform tin and press the dough into it. Top with the beaten egg and cheese strips. • Bake for 35 minutes. • Switch off the oven and leave the flan for a further 10 minutes. • Fill halved slices of salmon with quark and dill and arrange on top; garnish with dill.

Spring Green Quiche

Quantities for 1 26cm/11in springform tin:
150g/5½oz wheatmeal flour
150g/5oz butter
150g/5½oz low fat curd cheese
Pinch of salt
750g/1lb 11oz Swiss chard, turnip tops or spring greens
2 shallots
200g/7oz peeled, cooked prawns
½ tsp each of salt and freshly ground white pepper
Pinch of nutmeg
½ tsp grated lemon rind
A little lemon juice
125ml/4 fl oz cream
3 eggs
3 tbsps grated Parmesan cheese
Butter for the tin

Preparation time:
40 minutes
Standing time:
30 minutes
Baking time:
35 minutes
Nutritional value:
analysis per piece, if divided into 12 slices, approx:
• 840kJ/200kcal
• 8g protein
• 14g fat
• 11g carbohydrate

Knead the flour with 100g/4oz of the butter, the curd cheese and salt into a dough. Cover and refrigerate for 30 minutes. • Trim the leaves from the stalks of the greens, and cut the leaves into 1cm/½in strips. Blanch in boiling salted water for 5 seconds, plunge into cold water and leave to drain. Blanch the stalks for 1 minute. • Chop the shallots and fry in the rest of the butter until translucent. Add the stalks and fry for 3 minutes; combine with the prawns and leaves, and season with the salt and spices. • Butter a springform tin. Roll out the dough and line the tin with it, making a 4cm/2in high rim. Bake blind for 10 minutes in a preheated 200°C/400°F/Gas Mark 6 oven. • Beat the eggs with the cream and Parmesan. Pour the filling over the pastry case, then add the egg-and-cream mixture. • Bake for 35 minutes.

Rice Salad with Fish

To serve 8:
200g/7oz brown rice
500ml/16fl oz water
1 tsp salt
600g/1lb 6oz coley fillet
4 tbsps lemon juice
2 red onions
250g/8oz cucumber
250g/8oz tomatoes
250g/8oz sharp apples
3 tbsps sesame or soya oil
2 tsps garlic salt
1 tsp five-spice powder
4 tbsps finely chopped fresh dill
2 tbsps chopped chives

Preparation time:
1 hour
Marinating time:
1 hour
Nutritional value:
Analysis per serving, approx:
• 985kJ/235kcal
• 17g protein
• 7g fat
• 28g carbohydrate

Boil the rice over a gentle heat in a covered pan for 30 minutes. • Wash the fish and sprinkle it with 1 tbsp lemon juice and lay it on top of the rice. Tightly cover the pan and cook for a further 10 minutes until both rice and fish are tender. • Break the fish into pieces. Slice the onions into thin rings. Peel and dice the cucumber. Wash the tomatoes, remove the hard knot where the stalk joins the fruit and cut them into slices. Cut the apples into quarters, remove the cores and dice them. • Place all the ingredients in a large bowl, and sprinkle with the oil and remaining lemon juice. Add the garlic salt, five-spice powder and herbs and mix the salad carefully. • Leave for 1 hour to marinate before serving.

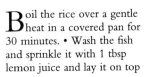

Millet Salad

100g/4oz millet
1 tsp salt
1 tsp finely chopped basil
250g/8oz cauliflower florets
100g/4oz cured pork slices
100g/4oz soft cheese
50g/2oz hazelnuts
2 hard-boiled eggs
4 tbsps orange juice
1 tbsp lemon juice
1 tbsp walnut oil
1 tbsp sherry
Pinch of lemon pepper
1 tbsp chopped chives

Preparation time:
30 minutes
Nutritional value:
Analysis per serving, approx:
• 1800kJ/430kcal
• 18g protein
• 29g fat
• 23g carbohydrate

Boil the millet for 15 minutes in 500ml/16fl oz water, salt and basil. • Rinse the cauliflower florets, add to the millet and cook for a further 10 minutes. • Cut the cheese and pork into strips and mix with the nuts, egg segments, the drained, cooled millet and cauliflower mixture. • Stir in the remaining ingredients and serve.

Oaten Salad

100g/4oz oats
1 tsp vegetable stock granules
75g/3oz blue cheese
2 tbsps red wine vinegar
1 tbsp safflower oil
1 tbsp concentrated apple juice
1 red apple
200g/7oz chicory
50g/2oz Camembert cheese

1 onion
50g/2oz sunflower seeds
2 tbsps chopped chives
Freshly ground black pepper

Preparation time:
1 hour
Nutritional value:
Analysis per serving, approx:
•1300kJ/310kcal
• 14g protein
• 16g fat
• 27g carbohydrate

Place the oats in 375ml/14 fl oz of water. Add the vegetable stock granules and boil for 50 minutes. • Crumble the blue cheese. Mix the vinegar, oil and apple juice. • Rinse and quarter the apple. Remove the core and cut into cubes. Rinse and trim the chicory and cut into strips. Cut the Camembert into cubes. Peel and chop the onion. • Mix all the prepared ingredients plus the sunflower seeds, drained oats and chopped chives with the cheese dressing. Season with pepper and serve.

Pearl Barley Salad

100g/4oz pearl barley
½ bay leaf
200g/7oz shelled peas
200g/7oz smoked tongue
1 tbsp parsley
1 tbsp chives
3 tbsps sour cream
2 tbsps safflower oil
1 tbsp cider vinegar
½ tsp celery salt

Soaking time:
12 hours
Preparation time:
45 minutes

Nutritional value:
Analysis per serving, approx:
• 1220kJ/290kcal
• 14g protein
• 14g fat
• 25g carbohydrate

Soak the pearl barley overnight in 500ml/16fl oz of water. • Boil 750ml/1¼ pints of fresh water with the bay leaf and cook the barley grains for 40 minutes until soft. Add the peas for the last 5 minutes. • Cut the tongue into thin strips. Drain the pearl barley and peas and stir in the remaining ingredients.

Bean Salad with Smoked Fish

To serve 10:
100g/4oz white haricot beans
100g/4oz black beans
100g/4oz aduki beans
2l/2½ pints water
1 bay leaf
2 tbsps vegetable stock granules
500g/1lb 2oz green beans
4 onions, 2 red and 2 white
500g/1lb 2oz green peppers
500g/1lb 2oz beefsteak tomatoes
500g/1lb 2oz smoked fish
4 tbsps sunflower oil
6 tbsps cider vinegar
Freshly ground black pepper
2 tsps garlic salt
2 tsps paprika
2 tsps mixed herbs
3 tbsps finely chopped fresh parsley

Soaking time:
12 hours
Preparation time:
1 hour
Marinating time:
30 minutes

Nutritional value:
Analysis per serving, approx:
• 1295kJ/310kcal
• 18g protein
• 17g fat
• 22g carbohydrate

Soak the beans in 1l/1¾ pints water overnight. • Drain them and boil in 1l/1¾ pints fresh water with the bay leaf and stock granules for 10 minutes. Wash the green beans and cut them into 4-5cm/1½-2-inch lengths and cook them with the other beans for a further 30 minutes over a gentle heat. • Drain the beans. Cut the onions into rings and the peppers into strips. Wash and dry the tomatoes, then cut them into eighths. Slice the smoked fish thickly. Make a marinade of the remaining ingredients. Mix the prepared salad ingredients together with the marinade. • Leave for at least 30 minutes before serving.

Millet Pancakes with Asparagus and Ham

250ml/9fl oz water
Salt
100g/4oz millet
60ml/2fl oz milk
500g/1lb 2oz green asparagus
2 eggs
50ml/2fl oz double cream
Sea salt and freshly ground
white pepper
½ tsp curry powder
20g/3/4oz butter
1 tbsp snipped chives
100g/4oz smoked ham, thinly
sliced
2 tbsps white wine vinegar
2 tbsps safflower oil
2 tbsps finely chopped fresh
herbs (such as parsley, dill,
tarragon and lemon balm)
1 hard-boiled egg, shelled

Preparation time:
50 minutes
Nutritional value:
Analysis per serving, approx:
• 1890kJ/450kcal
• 20g protein
• 31g fat
• 25g carbohydrate

Bring the water to the boil.
Add a pinch of salt and the
millet, and simmer for 15
minutes. Add the milk and
cook for a further 5 minutes.
Remove from the heat and
leave to soak for 10 minutes. •
Peel the asparagus and remove
the woody ends. Place in a
pan, cover with water, and
simmer for about 15 minutes.
Drain thoroughly. • Beat the
eggs with the cream, sea salt to
taste and the curry powder,
and add to the millet. • Melt
the butter in a pan, shape the
millet mixture into 4 pancakes
and fry. Put one on each of
four plates, and sprinkle over
the chives. • Wrap the ham
slices round the asparagus
spears and arrange on the
plates. • Beat together the
vinegar, oil and herbs, and
season to taste with sea salt and
pepper. Finely chop the egg
and add it to the dressing.
Serve the pancakes and hand
the dressing separately.

Prawns on Toast with Béarnaise Sauce

1 shallot
3 sprigs fresh tarragon or 1 tsp dried tarragon
3 tbsps white wine vinegar
5 white peppercorns
75g/3oz butter
3 egg yolks
Salt
Pinch sugar
300g/10oz prawns
1 tsp lemon juice
4 slices thick-cut bread
1 lemon

Preparation time:
40 minutes
Nutritional value:
Analysis per serving, approx:
• 1300kJ/310kcal
• 17g protein
• 22g fat
• 13g carbohydrate

Peel and chop the shallot. Rinse and dry the fresh tarragon. Remove the leaves from the stems and chop finely, but reserve a few for the garnish. Place the shallot, half the chopped tarragon, vinegar and peppercorns in a saucepan, boil and leave to stand for 3 minutes. • Melt 50g/2oz butter. Pour the egg yolks into a small saucepan. Place the small saucepan inside a larger pan filled with hot water. Beat the eggs until frothy and then slowly add the melted butter. Finally add the tarragon liquid and the rest of the chopped tarragon leaves. Season this Béarnaise sauce with the salt and sugar and take the small saucepan out of the hot water. • If necessary, de-vein the prawns, rinse in cold water and sprinkle with lemon juice. • Heat the grill. • Toast the bread and spread with the remaining butter. Arrange the prawns on the toast and pour over the sauce. Leave under the grill for 2 to 3 minutes. • Garnish with lemon slices and the reserved tarragon leaves.

Turkey on Toast

4 slices thick-cut bread
1 tbsp mayonnaise (50% fat content)
200g/7oz smoked turkey breasts cut into thin slices
8 soft, stoned prunes
4 thick slices Havarti or Tilsit cheese (about 150g/5-6oz)
2 thin rashers rindless bacon
2 tsps cranberry jelly

Preparation time:
20 minutes
Nutritional value:
Analysis per serving, approx:
• 1700kJ/400kcal
• 25g protein
• 23g fat
• 24g carbohydrate

Heat the oven to 220°C/450°F/gas mark 7 or turn on the grill. • Toast the bread, coat with mayonnaise and cover with turkey slices. Halve the prunes and place four halves on each slice. Remove the rind from the cheese and place one slice on top of the prunes. Bake in the oven or under the grill for 5 - 8 minutes until the cheese begins to melt. •Halve the bacon rashers and fry without fat until brown and crisp. Soak up any fat with kitchen paper. • Arrange the toast on plates and top each one with two half rashers of bacon and half a teaspoon of cranberry jelly. • Serve the turkey toast hot. Mixed pickles, gherkins, cocktail onions or pickled beetroot make good accompaniments.

Our tip: *Instead of turkey, try pork ribs or smoked tongue. Dust with a little paprika rather than cranberry jelly.*

40

Liver Pâté and Pears on Toast

4 slices thick-cut bread
4 canned pear halves
4 slices duck liver pâté
(50g/2oz each)
4 tsps cranberry jelly
4 slices Cheshire cheese
(100g/4oz)
2 thin rashers rindless bacon
(25g/1oz)
Some sprigs parsley

Preparation time:
25 minutes
Nutritional value:
Analysis per serving, approx:
• 2090kJ/500kcal
• 22g protein
• 31g fat
• 32g carbohydrate

Heat the oven to
200°C/400°F/gas mark 6.
• Toast the bread. Drain the
canned pear halves. Spread the
pâté on each slice of toast and
add a teaspoon of cranberry
jelly to the middle of each one
and then cover with the pear
halves. Cut the rind off the
cheese and arrange carefully on
top of the pear halves. • Bake
the toast in the oven on the
middle shelf for about 8
minutes or until the cheese
begins to melt. • In the
meantime brown both sides of
the bacon in a frying pan
without fat until crisp and
brown. Rinse the parsley sprigs
and shake dry. • Serve the toast
hot with half a bacon rasher
and a sprig of parsley.

Our tip: *If you would prefer to
use fresh pears, then they should
be halved, peeled and cored. Poach
them for 10 minutes over a gentle
heat in 125ml\4fl oz water or
white wine with 2 tablespoons of
lemon juice and 1 tablespoon of
sugar, then leave to cool. A
smooth calf's liver pâté may be
used instead of duck liver pâté and
redcurrant jelly instead of cranberry
jelly.*

41

Soufflé Omelettes with Liver and Mushroom Filling

For the filling:
200g/7oz chicken livers
250g/8oz button mushrooms
1 onion
30g/1oz butter
Salt and freshly ground black pepper
1 tbsp flour
Sprig of tarragon
4 tbsps dry sherry
For the omelettes:
6 eggs
Salt
45g/1½oz butter

Preparation time:
45 minutes
Nutritional value:
Analysis per serving, approx:
• 1590kJ/380kcal
• 22g protein
• 26g fat
• 6g carbohydrate

Gently rinse the chicken livers under the cold tap and then pat dry. • Rinse and trim the mushrooms. Dry and slice them finely. Peel and chop the onion. • Heat a knob of butter and fry the chopped onion until soft. Add the mushrooms and season with salt and pepper. Continue to cook for 5 minutes, stirring frequently. • Cut the livers into small pieces, dust with flour and fry lightly with a further knob of butter. Add the sherry and set aside. • Rinse the tarragon. Dry well and chop finely. Add the chopped tarragon and browned chicken livers to the mushrooms. Season again with salt and pepper. • To prepare the omelettes, separate the eggs. Whisk the egg whites with 2 tablespoons water and some salt until stiff. Beat the egg yolks and fold into the egg white with the whisk. • Heat the butter and make four omelettes from the egg mixture over a medium heat. Keep the omelettes warm until they are all cooked. Spoon in the liver filling, fold over and serve at once.

42

Spicy Fried Eggs

2 onions
1 garlic clove
1 red pepper
4 small tomatoes
1 tbsp olive oil
8 rashers rindless bacon (about 100g/4oz)
12 stuffed olives
Freshly ground black pepper
4 eggs
Salt
2 pinches paprika
1 tbsp chopped chives

Preparation time:
25 minutes
Nutritional value:
Analysis per serving, approx:
• 1500kJ/360kcal
• 11g protein
• 31g fat
• 10g carbohydrate

Peel the onion and cut into thin rings. Chop the garlic clove very finely. Quarter the pepper and remove the seeds and pith. Rinse, dry and cut into thin strips. Score the skin of the tomatoes and immerse in boiling water for a few seconds. Skin, remove the stalks and cut each one into eight segments. • Heat the oil in a large saucepan and fry the bacon. Add the strips of sweet pepper, onion rings, garlic and tomato segments. Cook everything over a gentle heat for about 5 minutes. • Cut the olives into slices and add to the saucepan. Season with pepper. Break the eggs into a cup one at a time and pour them gently into the pan. Cover the pan and fry the eggs for 5-10 minutes or until cooked. • Before serving, season with salt and paprika and sprinkle with the chopped chives. Serve at once.

Baked Eggs with Prawns

250g/8oz prawns
8 eggs
5 tbsps single cream
Salt and freshly ground white
pepper
½ tsp paprika
2 dill leaves
Butter for greasing

Preparation time:
20 minutes
Nutritional value:
Analysis per serving, approx:
• 1000kJ/240kcal
• 23g protein
• 17g fat
• 1g carbohydrate

Heat the oven to 200°C/400°F/gas mark 6.
• If necessary, de-vein the prawns. Rinse the prawns in a sieve and leave to drain. • Beat the eggs in a bowl with the cream, salt, pepper and paprika, then stir in the prawns. • Grease the insides of four ovenproof ramekins with butter and spoon in the beaten eggs. • Place the ramekins on the middle shelf of the oven for 10 minutes. • Rinse and dry the dill and place on top of the dish as a garnish. • Serve with French bread, garlic butter and a dry white wine.

Our tip: If you would prefer not to use the oven to save energy, the eggs can be fried in a frying pan. Fry three finely chopped shallots in butter until soft, add the prawns and then the seasoned beaten egg. Cook for about 5 minutes over a gentle heat. Serve on warmed plates and sprinkle with chopped chives.

Pasta and Vegetable Salad

To serve 6:
2 l/3½ pints water
Salt and freshly ground black pepper
250g/8oz macaroni
250g/8oz carrots
250g/8oz green beans
3 tomatoes
300g/10oz frozen peas
2 small courgettes
3 tbsps mayonnaise
200ml/7fl oz soured cream
3 tbsps cider vinegar
Pinch of sugar
1 bunch of parsley
1 bunch of chives

Preparation time:
45 minutes
Standing time:
30 minutes
Nutritional value:
Analysis per serving, approx:
• 1380kJ/330kcal
• 14g protein
• 8g fat
• 52g carbohydrate

Bring the water to the boil in a large pan. Add ½ tsp salt and the pasta, and cook for 8-10 minutes until tender but still firm to the bite. Drain, rinse with cold water and drain again. • Wash, peel and dice the carrots. Top and tail, wash and chop the beans. Put the beans and carrots in a pan of lightly salted boiling water, bring back to the boil and cook for 15 minutes. • Wash and dry the tomatoes, and cut into eight. • Place the peas in a small pan, just cover with water and add a pinch of salt. Bring to the boil, and simmer for 5 minutes. • Trim, wash, dry and slice the courgettes. • Mix together the mayonnaise, soured cream, vinegar, and sugar, and season to taste with salt and pepper. Wash the parsley and chives and shake dry. Finely chop the parsley, and add it to the dressing. • Drain the cooked vegetables and leave to cool. • Place the pasta, carrots, beans, tomatoes, peas and courgettes in a salad

46

bowl. Pour over the dressing. •
Snip the chives and sprinkle
them over the salad. Cover
and leave to stand for 30
minutes.

Chef's Salad

250g/8oz boneless turkey breast
1 tbsp oil
Salt and freshly ground white pepper
1 lettuce
200g/7oz radicchio
150ml/5fl oz soured cream
3 tbsps mayonnaise
1-2 tbsps tomato ketchup
1 tsp Dijon mustard
1 tbsp lemon juice
Pinch of sugar
1 small onion
125g/5oz Edam cheese
125g/5oz cooked ham
4 hard-boiled eggs, shelled

Preparation time:
30 minutes
Nutritional value:
Analysis per serving, approx:
• 2180kJ/520kcal
• 45g protein
• 34g fat
• 8g carbohydrate

Wash the turkey breast and pat dry. Heat the oil in a pan, and fry the turkey over a moderate heat for 4-5 minutes on each side. Season to taste with salt and pepper, remove from the pan and leave to cool. • Trim and wash the lettuce and radicchio, then shake dry. • Beat together the soured cream, mayonnaise, ketchup, mustard, lemon juice and sugar. Peel and mince the onion, and stir it into the dressing. • Cut the cheese into 3cm/1-inch strips. Cut the ham into 3cm/1-inch strips. Slice the eggs and the turkey breast. • Arrange the lettuce and radicchio leaves on a large, flat serving platter or divide between four individual plates. Arrange the turkey breast, ham, cheese and eggs decoratively on top. Pour the dressing over the salad or serve separately.

Damson Flan

Quantities for 1 28cm/11in
springform tin
250g/8oz flour
50g/2oz sugar
Generous pinch of salt
100g/4oz butter, diced
8 tbsps cold water
2 tsps vinegar
1kg/2¼lbs damsons
125ml/4 fl oz cream
2 eggs
Generous pinch of ground
cinnamon

Preparation time:
50 minutes
Baking time:
35 minutes
Nutritional value:
Analysis per slice, approx, if
divided into 12 slices:
• 1090kJ/260kcal
• 5g protein
• 12g fat
• 33g carbohydrate

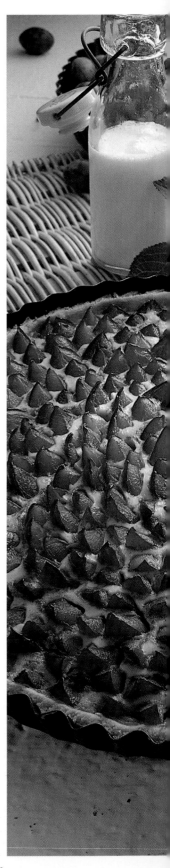

Mix the flour with 1 tbsp sugar, the salt, butter, water and vinegar. Make a dough using a food mixer or food processor, then use cold hands to make a smooth shortcrust dough. Wrap in clingfilm and leave in the refrigerator for 30 minutes to chill. • Rinse, drain, halve and stone the damsons. • Butter the tin. Heat the oven to 220°/450°F/Gas Mark 7. • Roll out the dough into a circle on a floured work top. Line the tin with the dough, pinching up a 2cm/1in rim. Arrange the damsons close together in a circular pattern on the dough, cut sides upwards. • Bake on the middle shelf of the oven for 10 minutes. • Stir the remaining sugar and cinnamon into the eggs and cream and pour this over the damsons. Bake for a further 25 minutes. If required, sprinkle a few sugar crystals over the cooled surface before serving.

Chocolate Vanilla Layer Cake

Quantities for 1 26cm/10in tin
5 eggs
½ tsp vanilla essence
150g/5½oz raw whole cane sugar
100g/4oz wholewheat flour
20g/½oz cornflour or arrowroot
1 tsp baking powder
100g/4oz coarsely grated plain chocolate
75g/3oz butter, melted
750ml/1½ pints milk
50g/2oz cornflour
½ tsp vanilla essence
50g/2oz butter
1 egg yolk
For the decoration:
200g/7oz blanched almonds
150g/51/2oz honey
1 tbsp rosewater
12 currants
50g/2oz cocoa powder

Preparation time:
2 hours
Baking time:
35 minutes
Nutritional value:
Analysis per slice, approx, if divided into 12 slices:
• 2100kJ/500kcal
• 14g protein
• 30g fat
• 43g carbohydrate

Beat the egg yolks with the vanilla, sugar and 2 tbsps warm water. Mix together the flour, cornflour, baking powder and chocolate and combine with the egg yolks. Whisk the whites until stiff. Fold them into the flour mixture with the butter. • Heat the oven to 180°C/350°F/Gas Mark 4. • Bake for 35 minutes, leave to cool and then slice the cakeinto three layers. Warm the remaining honey. • Whisk the milk with the cornflour and vanilla. Stir into the honey and boil briefly. • Mix together just under a third of the cooled filling with the butter and egg yolk. Spread the bottom and middle layers with the remaining filling while still warm. Re-assemble the cake. Spread the rest of the filling over the top. • The next day, make the marzipan. Grind the

almonds very finely and mix to
a paste in a bowl over
simmering water with
100g/4oz honey and the
rosewater. Sprinkle the top of
the cake thickly with cocoa
powder. • Roll out half the
marzipan to line the side of the
cake. Use marzipan and
currants to shape 12 flowers.

Boston Cream Pie

Quantities for 1 26cm/10in tin

For the cake mixture:
125g/5oz softened butter
325g/11oz sugar
4 eggs
250g/8oz flour
2 tsps baking powder
2 tbsps milk

For the filling:
3 lemons
100g/4oz sugar
3 tsps cornflour
500ml/18 fl oz whipping cream

Preparation time:
40 minutes
Baking time:
50 minutes
Nutritional value:
Analysis per slice, approx, if divided into 16 slices:
• 1510kJ/360kcal
• 6g protein
• 20g fat
• 42g carbohydrate

Cream the butter with 125g/5oz sugar. Separate the eggs. Combine the egg yolks with the flour, baking powder and milk and stir into the creamed butter. • Heat the oven to 200°C/400°F/Gas Mark 6. Line the base of the tin. Bake half of the mixture for 15 minutes. Whisk the egg whites with the remaining sugar and beat until stiff but not dry. Cover the baked cake base with half of the whisked egg whites. Bake for a further 10 minutes. Repeat the process using the remaining cake mixture and whisked egg whites. • Leave both bases to cool. • Squeeze the lemons and strain the juice. Mix the juice with 125ml/4 fl oz water and the sugar. Bring to the boil. Stir the cornflour to a paste with 4 tbsps cold water, add to the lemon juice and leave to cool. • Whip the cream until very stiff. Add the cold lemon mixture to the cream a spoonful at a time. Spread half the lemon cream over the bottom half of the cake, replace the upper layer and coat the top and sides with the remainder of the mixture. Serve immediately.

Wedding Cake

Quantities for 1 26cm/10in tin:

For the cake mixture:
250g/8oz softened butter
125g/5oz sugar
1 tbsp vanilla sugar
4 eggs
150g/5½oz each flour and cornflour
100g/4oz ground almonds
2 tsps baking powder

For the cream filling:
125g/5oz butter
125g/5oz sugar
4 egg yolks
2 lemons

For the icing and decoration:
1 egg white
250g/8oz icing sugar
2 tbsps lemon juice
30g/1oz chopped pistachio nuts
16 candied violets

Preparation time:
80 minutes
Baking time:
45 minutes

Nutritional value:
Analysis per slice, approx, if divided into 16 slices:
• 2010kJ/480kcal
• 7g protein
• 27g fat
• 53g carbohydrate

Cream the butter with the sugar and vanilla sugar. Add four eggs and 4 tbsps water. • Mix together the flour, baking powder, almonds and cornflour. Stir into the creamed butter. • Heat the oven to 180°C/350°F/Gas Mark 4. • Bake for 45 minutes. • Melt the butter and add the sugar and egg yolks. Grate the rind from one lemon and squeeze the juice from both. Add both to the melted butter. Beat in a bain-marie until creamy. • When the cake has cooled, cut into three layers. Spread the bottom and middle layers with the lemon cream and then re-assemble the cake, adding the top slice. • Whisk the egg white until stiff. Mix in the icing sugar and lemon juice. Ice the cake. When the icing has almost set, decorate with piped icing, pistachios and violets.

Grape Tartlets

*Quantities for 8 12cm/5in
tartlets*

**For the sweet shortcrust
dough:**
*300g/10oz flour
150g/5½oz butter
100g/4oz sugar
1 tbsp vanilla sugar
Pinch of salt
1 egg yolk*
For the filling:
*1 packet unflavoured gelatine
3 eggs
100g/4oz icing sugar
125ml/4 fl oz marsala
2 tbsps lemon juice
300g/10oz each green and
black grapes
50g/2oz toasted, flaked
almonds*

Preparation time:
1¾ hours
Baking time:
20 minutes
Nutritional value:
Analysis per tartlet, approx:
• 2310kJ/550kcal
• 12g protein
• 25g fat
• 68g carbohydrate

Mix together the
ingredients for the
dough. Knead well, cover with
clingfilm and chill for 1 hour. •
Dissolve the gelatine in
125ml/4 fl oz hot water.
Separate the eggs. Pour
sufficient water into a large
saucepan for it to come
5cm/2in up the sides. Put the
egg yolks and icing sugar into
a mixing bowl and beat them
over the water . Stir in the
marsala. Warm the lemon juice
and add it to the yolks. Add
the gelatine and mix well.
Whisk the egg whites until stiff
but not dry and then fold into
the egg yolk mixture with a
spoon. Leave this custard in
the refrigerator for 1 hour to
set, stirring occasionally. • Heat
the oven to 200°C/400°F/Gas
Mark 6. • Butter the tartlet
tins. Divide the dough into
eight equal parts. Roll it into
thin sheets and use them to
line the tins. Prick the dough
with a fork and trim off any
excess. Bake the tartlets blind
for 20 minutes or until golden

brown. • Wash the grapes and remove any stalks. • Spoon the wine custard into the tartlets. Top with grapes and sprinkle flaked almonds around the rims.

57

Amaretto Sponges

Quantities for 60 sponges
5 egg yolks
125g/5oz sugar
5 egg whites
Juice of 1 orange
75g/3oz flour
50g/2oz potato starch
125ml/4 fl oz amaretto
200g/7oz apricot jam
100g/4oz flaked almonds
Non-stick baking paper for the baking sheet

Preparation time:
20 minutes
Baking time:
8 minutes
Completion time:
20 minutes
Nutritional value:
Analysis per serving, approx:
• 210kJ/50kcal
• 2g protein
• 2g fat
• 6g carbohydrate

Preheat the oven to 200°C/400°F/Gas Mark 6.

Line the baking sheet with non-stick baking paper. • Cream the yolks with 75g/3oz sugar. • Beat the egg whites with the remaining sugar and 1 tsp orange juice into stiff peaks. Fold this into the yolk mixture. Sift the flour and baking powder over the mixture. Fold it in lightly. • Spread the sponge mixture over the baking sheet. Bake for 8 minutes on the middle shelf until golden. • Turn out the sponge, and remove the paper. Using a glass about 4cm/1½in in diameter, press out overlapping crescents. • Mix the remaining orange juice with the liqueur and brush this over the crescents, until they are saturated. • Mix the jam with 1-2 tbsps hot water, strain and brush over the crescents. • Toast the flaked almonds in a dry frying-pan until golden, and sprinkle over the crescents. • Wrap them in foil and chill until ready to serve.

Pumpkin Tartlets

Quantities for 10 tartlets
200g/7oz flour
100g/4oz butter, cut into
small pieces
100g/4oz sugar
6 egg yolks
1 tbsp crème fraîche
500g/1lb2oz cooked pumpkin,
peeled and seeded
¼ tsp ground cinnamon
Grated rind of 1 lemon
¼ tsp freshly grated nutmeg

Preparation time:
45 minutes
Standing time:
1 hour
Baking time:
30 minutes
Nutritional value:
Analysis per serving, approx:
• 1800kJ/430kcal
• 12g protein
• 29g fat
• 28g carbohydrate

Sift the flour into a bowl and sprinkle with the butter.

Add half the sugar, 2 of the egg yolks and the crème fraîche. Knead to a firm dough. • Wrap the dough in clingfilm and chill for 1 hour. • Cut the pumpkin into small cubes. Reserve one quarter and purée the remainder. Mix the remaining 4 yolks, the remaining sugar, the cinnamon, the lemon peel and the nutmeg with the purée. Fold in the cubed pumpkin. • Preheat the oven to 180°C/350°F/Gas Mark 4. • Roll out the dough to a 5mm/⅛in-thick sheet. Cut out 10 little shapes, each 7cm/2½in in diameter. Bake for about 10 minutes on the middle shelf of the oven. • Fill the cases with the pumpkin purée and bake for another 20 minutes until golden. • Allow the tartlets to cool first of all in the moulds, then on a cake rack.

Nougat Cornets

Quantities for 30 cornets
5 sheets of extra-strong gold
foil (from craft suppliers)
40 shelled hazelnuts
4 tbsps cream
100g/4oz plain chocolate
coating
200g/7oz nougat
1 tbsp butter

Preparation time:
1½ hours
Cooling time:
1 hour
Nutritional value:
Analysis per serving, approx:
• 330kJ/80kcal
• 1g protein
• 4g fat
• 5g carbohydrate

Preheat the oven to
225°C/437°F/Gas Mark 7.
• Take the gold foil and cut
out 30 circles, each 6cm/2¼in
in diameter. Shape them into
pointed cones. • Sprinkle the
hazelnuts onto a baking sheet.
Roast for 5 minutes in the
oven until the brown skins
burst open. • Rub the nuts in a
dry cloth until all the skins are
removed. Cut 15 nuts in half,
finely chop the remainder. •
Warm the cream on a low
heat. Break up the chocolate
coating. Add to the cream and
melt, stirring. Remove from
the heat. • Break up the
nougat into small pieces. Add
to the butter and the chopped
nuts, and gradually combine
with the coating. • Place the
pan in a bowl of iced water.
Whisk the mixture until cold
and frothy. • Fit a star-shaped
nozzle onto a piping bag. Fill
the bag with the nougat
mixture. Pipe the mixture into
the cornets, rounding off each
one with a rosette. Put half a
nut onto each rosette. •
Refrigerate the cornets for 1
hour. Store in a cool place.

Andalusian Egg Creams

Quantities for 50 creams
300g/10oz sugar
3 tbsps medium-dry sherry
Grated rind of 1 orange
7 egg yolks
100g/4oz icing sugar, sifted
50 sweet cases

Preparation time:
1 hour
Nutritional value:
Analysis per serving, approx:
• 350kJ/83kcal
• 2g protein
• 5g fat
• 8g carbohydrate

Put the sherry and the sugar into a pan. Melt on medium heat to a brown syrup, stirring constantly. Add the orange rind and mix in. • With a whisk, or in an electric blender, beat the egg yolks until creamy and frothy. • Slowly trickle in the warm syrup, stirring all the time, until the ingredients are well mixed. • Allow the mixture to cool. Shape into a roll, about 2cm/¾in in diameter. Cut into 2cm/¾in slices and shape them into balls. • Sift the icing sugar onto a dish. Carefully roll the balls in it. Put them into the sweet cases. Store in the refrigerator until serving.

Spanish Nougat

Quantities for 70 diamonds
3 egg whites
225g/7½oz honey
150g/5½oz sugar
4 tbsps vanilla sugar
100g/4oz grated hazelnuts
100g/4oz grated almonds
100g/4oz grated pine nut kernels
8-10 large rectangular baking wafers

Preparation time:
45 minutes
Standing time:
12 hours
Nutritional value:
Analysis per serving, approx:
• 210kJ/50kcal
• 1g protein
• 3g fat
• 6g carbohydrate

Beat the egg whites until very firm. • Add the honey, and then sprinkle or drizzle in the sugar and the vanilla sugar, beating constantly. Stir the mixture until viscous. • Turn the mixture into a saucepan. Warm on very low heat and stir until the mixture comes away from the base. This will require patience. • Gradually add the grated nuts. Continue stirring until the ingredients are well mixed. • Arrange half the wafers in a loaf-tin or in a 4cm/1½in-high springform cake-tin. • Put the nut mixture onto each one, spread smooth and top with the remaining wafers. • Leave to set for 12 hours. Then cut into small lozenges.

Index

Amaretto Sponges 58

Andalusian Egg Creams 62

Baked Eggs with
Prawns 45

Bean Salad with Smoked
Fish 36

Beetroot Canapés 8

Boston Cream Pie 54

Caraway Rolls 19

Caviar Canapés 10

Cheese and Pine Nut
Pie 22

Chef's Salad 48

Chicken and Fennel
Tartlets 7

Chicken Strudel 26

Chocolate Vanilla Layer
Cake 52

Coriander Straws 14

Cottage Cheese and Herb
Canapés 9

Cottage Cheese on
Cucumber Slices 16

Cottage Cheese with
Herbs on French Bread
Boats 17

Damson Flan 50

Garlic Croûtons 10

Grape Tartlets 56

Ham Croissants 18

Liver Pâté and Pears on
Toast 41

Maatjes Herring
Cocktail 24

Millet Pancakes with
Asparagus and Ham 37

Millet Salad 34

Nougat Cornets 60

Oaten Salad 34

Olive Tapas 11

Pasta and Vegetable
Salad 46

Pearl Barley Salad 35

Prawns on Toast with
Béarnaise Sauce 38

Pumpkin Tartlets 59

Rice Salad with Fish 33

Salmon Flan with
Cheese 31

Sauerkraut Pie 23

Soufflé Omelettes with
Liver and Mushroom
Filling 42

Spanish Nougat 63

Spicy Fried Eggs 44

Spinach and Cod Flan 30

Spring Green Quiche 32

Stuffed Eggs 12

Stuffed Turkey Fillet 20

Suffed Salmon Rolls 24

Thyme Wafers 15

Trout Pâté en Croûte 28

Turkey on Toast 40

Wedding Cake 55